Stranger Danger - How to Talk to Kids About Strangers

KRISTI PORTER

ISBN-10: 0615890431 ISBN-13: 978-0615890432

DEDICATION

Early in my teaching career, while putting together a unit about child safety for my class, I came across a statistic that stated: "In the majority of small child, stranger kidnapping cases, the child is simply taken by the hand and led quietly away." I wasn't sure that I agreed with that statistic, and decided to put it to the test.

With the parents' permission, I arranged to conduct a simple 'stranger test' at the annual springtime family picnic. This experiment really opened my eyes about how young children view strangers, and why Stranger Danger Programs often fail. Since that day twenty-five years ago, I've made it my mission to help teach young kids to stay safe.

I've used the methods in this book with hundreds of kids ages 3-7, and I'm happy to report that many of my earliest students (who are now adults) tell me that they still remember the lessons they learned about strangers, and want to know how to use those same methods to teach their children how to stay safe.

So it is for those first students, now parents themselves, that I've put this book together.

CONTENTS

A NOTE TO PARENTS

While statistics show that children are in more danger from those they know than from strangers, as a preschool teacher for over twenty years, it has been my experience that both parents and children continue to fear stranger abductions the most.

Thus *Stranger Danger - How to Talk to Kids About Strangers* is deliberately kept very narrow in scope, providing the essential elements for creating a framework of safety while maintaining a young child's feeling of security in the world. It is aimed at parents and caregivers of children ages 3-7, and is meant to be the beginning of an ongoing discussion between parents and children about the importance of personal safety.

In the following pages I will give you the tools you need to talk openly with young children about strangers and personal safety, without frightening them. Using a series of short, parent-child sessions spread out over the course of several days, I'll show you how to teach your child to stay safe, as well as how to help even the youngest of children learn how to handle tough situations. These tools are aimed at giving kids the knowledge and confidence to know what to do, and who to trust in a variety of different situations.

Young children learn best through play, and the methods used in this book are designed to be fun for the child. Each parent-child discussion or exercise should last no longer than 15-20 minutes. Most importantly, parents should put away their 'parent voice', and strive for more of a light-hearted, sometimes silly, and almost conspiratorial approach with their kids.

Keeping kids safe is a serious matter, but teaching children the skills they need to stay safe should be fun. Make it engaging, keep it positive, and enjoy the adventure.

1
THE STORY BEHIND THIS BOOK

Early in my teaching career, while putting together a unit about child safety for my class, I came across a statistic that stated: "In the majority of small child, stranger kidnapping cases, the child is simply taken by the hand and led quietly away." I wasn't sure that I agreed with that statistic, and decided to put it to the test.

With the parents' permission, I arranged to conduct a simple 'stranger test' at the annual springtime family picnic. Held at a popular local playground, twenty-four children (ages 2-8) and their parents attended. While the assistant teachers supervised the children, I called the parents aside and explained how the 'stranger test' would work.

An adult unknown to the children would simply walk up to them, take their hand and lead them away toward the parking lot. If the child asked where they were going, the 'stranger' would simply tell them there was some candy in the car, and that the child could have some if they wanted it. When they reached the car, (in full view of the playground and parents) the 'stranger' would simply tell the child that they ran out of candy, show them an empty candy bag, and return the child to the playground. If at any time the child resisted or became frightened, the 'stranger' would immediately let go and move away.

The parents were to stay on the sidelines and observe, agreeing to not punish their child if indeed they did walk away with one of the 'strangers'. This was to be a teachable moment - one that children, parents, and teachers would all discuss together at the end of the day. While many of the parents commented they didn't think their child would ever walk away with someone they didn't know, all agreed to allow their child to participate.

I called in my 'stranger' volunteers - one young adult male, and one middle aged female. Both were teachers in another program and unknown to the children or their parents.

I stood with the parents at the edge of the playground and watched with astonishment as one by one, almost half of the children simply walked away with one of the strangers!

Over the course of an afternoon, 11 children

accompanied a 'stranger' to the car - with no resistance, not even a glance back over their shoulder. They simply held hands and walked away - for nothing more than the promise of candy. Of the remaining children, only one became visibly frightened and was immediately returned to their parent. The others simply pulled their hand away and ran off to play with their friends. Only four of them reported the 'stranger' to a teacher or parent.

This experiment really opened my eyes about how young children view strangers, and why Stranger Danger Programs often fail. Since that day twenty-five years ago, I've made it my mission to help teach young kids to stay safe. I've used the methods in this book with hundreds of kids ages 3-7, and I'm happy to report that many of my earliest students (who are now adults) tell me that they still remember the lessons they learned about strangers, and want to know how to use those same methods to teach *their* children how to stay safe.

So it is for those first students, now parents themselves, that I've put this book together.

2
STRANGER DANGER

Parents tell their kids not to talk to strangers. They read stories to their children about not talking to strangers. They may even practice with their child what to do if approached by a stranger. But most parents never explain to their kids exactly who or what a stranger actually is.

When you sit down for dinner tonight, ask your child what a stranger looks like. Their answer will probably be some version of – "a bad guy." Ask them what a bad guy looks like, and you'll most likely hear – "I don't know, maybe like a monster, or a guy with a scary face."

Some kids may have an idea in their heads about what a stranger looks like. It quite often manifests itself into something they fear - be it monsters, bad guys, or even wild animals. Some kids may answer with "I don't know," and that's ok too, because the truth is:

Young children often don't understand
that a stranger is a regular person,
just someone that they don't know.

Read that line again, and highlight it. It is one of two fundamental reasons why so many Stranger Danger programs for young children fail.

Think about the storybooks your parents read to you growing up. Anytime there was a stranger mentioned, it was always depicted as a monster, or an animal, (remember the big bad wolf?) or occasionally a bad guy - complete with dark clothes and a mask. Never were ordinary people depicted as strangers. Why? It was thought that being truthful about strangers would only frighten young children, and make them fearful of everyone they met.

Fast forward twenty five years, and guess what? Today's storybooks are only slightly better. Is it any wonder that little kids have no clue about real strangers?

Now think about everything your parents told you about strangers. Don't talk to them, don't take candy from them, and don't get in a car with them. That about sum it up? Are you telling your children the same things?

In an attempt to keep their children safe from strangers, parents almost always warn their child about what NOT to do. Very few parents teach their children what they CAN do if they find themselves in a dangerous situation. Therein lays the second fundamental reason many Stranger Danger programs for young children fail:

Young children don't know
what they CAN do
when encountering a stranger.

Go ahead, highlight that line - we'll come back to it later. But first, let's take a look at how to make sure your child knows how to identify a stranger.

3
WHO IS A STRANGER?

If you have not yet asked your child what a stranger looks like, do so now. Their answer will give you some insight into their level of understanding and fear, and is your starting point for the rest of this discussion.

Whatever your child's answer, don't negate it. Agree that monsters or bad guys (or whatever other variation they have) are scary. Ask them to tell you about the scariest monster or bad guy they know about. Some kids won't have a lot to say, but others may go on in great detail, and that's ok. Nod along, listen, and let them talk. Don't interrupt. They are giving you inside information about their feelings, and their fears.

When they've finished talking, acknowledge what they've told you with a simple statement such as "Wow, that sounds like a really scary monster." (or bad guy/animal/etc.)

Then lean in close and whisper, "You know what?" At this point most kids become wide eyed, look straight at you, and want to know what you have to say.

You then lean back, and with a surprised look on your face say "Strangers are not monsters!" (or "not all strangers are bad guys!") As the look on their face becomes one of surprise, you can add incredulously, "I know! Isn't that crazy?!"

This wee bit of dramatics on your part draws the child in. Suddenly it's not a 'talk' or a lecture for them. It's a conversation.

Follow this by explaining that strangers are real people. They can be ladies or men, they can be old like a grandpa, or young like a teenager. They can even be kids! Explain that strangers are simply real people that the child doesn't know.

Then sit down and look through any magazine together. Ask them to point out all the pictures they see of strangers (or bad guys). Most won't pick any. Thumb through the magazine with your child again, but this time point to a few of the advertisements and ask your child if they know the person in the picture. While a few of the older children may answer "yes, that's the lady/man from the commercial on TV," most kids will answer no. Explain to your child that you don't know that person either, and move on to another picture. (For those that do answer yes, ask them if they know that person 'in real life.')

After several such interactions, close the
magazine and ask if any of those people
looked like monsters or bad guys. Then
explain to your child that all of the people in
those pictures were strangers, and ask them if
they know why. Give them plenty time to
think about it. If needed you can prompt them
with the question… "Do you know any of the
people in those pictures?" When they answer
no, you reply "and a stranger is somebody that
you don't know, right?" When they agree, give
a smile and a high five. Tell them to be sure to
remember that, because you're going to ask
them again later about strangers. Then turn
them loose to go play.

Wait no longer than a minute, before finding
them again and asking, "so… let's see if you
remember. What is a stranger?" When they
answer "somebody I don't know," get excited,
give a high five, and with a smile, tell them to
remember that, because you're going to ask
them again later.

Wait at least an hour before asking again,
and remember, your reaction to their correct
answer of "somebody I don't know" is key. It
makes it fun for the child, and your reminder

of "don't forget...I'm going to ask you again later," (said with a smile of course!) makes it feel like a game.

Ask them again at bedtime, and after giving the appropriate response for their correct answer, tell them to try and remember that answer all the way until morning, because you're going to ask them again at breakfast.

If your child doesn't remember the correct response of "somebody I don't know" the following morning, go back to the magazine pictures step and repeat it. Then ask your child what a stranger is several times throughout the day, rewarding each correct answer with excitement, high fives, and a smile. Don't make it a test, keep it fun. At bedtime, remind them that you are going to ask them again in the morning, and that they should try really hard to remember that a stranger is "somebody I don't know."

When your child is able to give the correct answer the following morning, kick the dramatics into high gear. Woo-who, do the happy dance, give high fives, get knuckles, or do whatever is right for you, to get your child to smile, or better yet, laugh at your antics. Encourage your child to join in, and praise them for remembering such important stuff.

4
GOOD STRANGERS

Now that your child understands that a stranger is "somebody I don't know", it's time to help them understand the difference between good strangers and bad strangers.

Start by asking your child, "Did you know there are two kinds of strangers?" Then go on to explain (add your own dramatics!) that there are Good Strangers and Bad Strangers, but kids have to be very careful about *all* strangers because you can't tell just by looking at someone if they are good or bad. Some Bad Strangers might look nice, and some Good Strangers may look very different from the child.

Ask your child, "So...who is a Good Stranger?" Some kids will answer with "I don't know." Others may have a few ideas, so give them plenty of time to think, and then listen to their answer. These are the people your child feels are safe. Are they the right people?

Explain to your child that Good strangers

are people you can go to if you need help. People like a policeman, a doctor, a teacher, a checkout clerk, etc. Use personal experiences or examples from your child's life here if possible; maybe talk about a recent visit to the emergency room, and how the doctor there was a Good Stranger, or how the policeman was a Good Stranger when he helped mom get her keys out of her locked car. If you can make it relevant to your child, it will stick with them.

Finish by again asking, "So…who is a Good Stranger?" Most kids will answer with a list of Good Strangers: policeman, doctor, etc. That's good, and they are right. Excitement, high fives and smiles all around!

If your child answers with "somebody I can go to if I need help", that's ok too, and usually the answer of an older child. Either way, break out the happy dance - you've done an awesome job. Now let's move on to Bad Strangers.

5
BAD STRANGERS

Kids need to know that Bad Strangers can be very tricky - and that's why they have to be so careful about *all* strangers. Explain (with dramatics, of course!) that sometimes a Bad Stranger may seem nice at first, but... then they try to trick kids!

Using simple terms, describe to your child several different ways that Bad Strangers may try to trick them. Some examples: A Bad Stranger might play tricks by saying that that they lost their kitty or puppy - *when they really didn't.* (Make sure to emphasize that last part - young children often don't 'get it' otherwise.) A Bad Stranger might say that mom or dad told them to come pick you up - *when they really didn't.* A Bad Stranger might say they need your help - *but they really don't.* A Bad Stranger might even say they will give you candy or cookies if you go with them - *but they really won't.*

You can even ask your child if they can think of any different ways that a Bad Stranger might try to trick little kids. Give them time to think, and listen to their answers...they are giving you important information. Discuss with them every scenario they come up with.

Next, ask your child if they know *why* Bad Strangers sometimes try to trick kids. Again, give them time to think, and listen to their answers.

Some children may reply that the Bad Stranger is just playing a joke on them, or wants to play a game. Others may say they don't know why, or that Bad Strangers play tricks because it's fun. A few, usually the older kids, will say that Bad Strangers play tricks so they can hurt or steal little kids.

No matter what their answer, it's time to use your 'parent voice'. Tell your child, "Bad Strangers try to trick kids so they can hurt them." Most kids will be wide-eyed about now, so give them a hug and tell them it's ok to be scared of Bad Strangers, even moms and dads are scared of Bad Strangers sometimes. Some kids may ask why Bad Strangers want to hurt kids; simply tell them you don't know.

Then lighten the mood a bit and turn on the dramatics. Tell your child, "So....let's see how much you remember." Then ask the following questions: "What is a stranger?" (Somebody that I don't know.) High Five for the correct answer! "And…. Who is a Good Stranger?" (Somebody I can go to if I need help, OR list of 'good strangers'.) Correct answer, more high fives. And finally… "Who is a Bad Stranger?" (Somebody that tries to trick kids so they can hurt them.) Did they get all three answers right? Happy Dance and Hugs all around!

Repeat those questions over the next several days. When your child can answer them all correctly, you are ready to move on to the next section, where I'll show you how to help your child learn what they CAN do if they ever encounter a Bad Stranger.

6
WHAT KIDS CAN DO

Now that your child understands the difference between Good and Bad Strangers, it's time to help them learn what they CAN do if they find themselves confronted with a Bad Stranger.

I mentioned earlier the statistic I'd run across that stated in most small child, stranger kidnappings, the child is simply taken by the hand and led away. The second part of that statistic was that kids who walk quietly away often don't come home. But kids that fight - even little kids - sometimes get away. Because of this, during my annual Personal Safety presentations to preschoolers, I spend a lot of time helping kids learn and practice things they CAN do, and help them understand that they CAN fight back when confronted with a Bad Stranger.

Parents need to do the same with their children. Kids (and even adults) get scared when they don't know what to do. They may panic, cry, or even freeze-up; none of which will help them to escape a Bad Stranger intent on taking them. So always emphasize what your child CAN do. The confidence they gain by knowing they CAN do something when confronted by a Bad Stranger, may be the key that allows them to remain calm long enough to DO something, and draw the attention of someone who can help them.

Please note: this section is not a one-time lesson. You should plan on discussing, and practicing, the what-to-do scenarios with your child over and over again. You can (and should) update and change the scenarios as your child gets older, but remember practice is the key. Once is not enough.

~~~~~~~~~~

Pick a day when your child is well rested and full of energy for this next session, and start by reviewing the earlier lessons about strangers with your child. When you are confident they understand, ask them if they'd like to play a pretend game called *Stranger-What If*. It's okay if they say no, some kids take a little longer than others to be comfortable with all the 'stranger' talk. Simply say okay, and mention you'd like to play it with them later. Then move on to another activity. Remember to ask again later - or maybe even the next day - if they'd like to play.

Once your child is agreeable, explain that *Stranger-What If* is a pretend game. Tell them you are going to ask them some questions, and then you are going to pretend to be a Bad Stranger and see if you can trick them. It's their job not to get tricked!

Start with the simple question: "What if *somebody you don't know* asks you to help them find their lost puppy? What do you do?" Most kids will answer "tell them no," but that's only partly correct. Explain (with dramatics of course!) they need to say no very loudly! (This is extremely important - it is intended to draw the attention of others nearby.) Then have your child practice saying "NO!" a few times as loud as they can. When you've had all the practice you can handle, smile and tell them "Okay, that's the first thing you do. But... (add your own dramatics!) then you need to run away, like this..." At this point you should run across the room - don't walk fast, jog, or stroll - Run! Then say, "and... you have to tell a grown up *right away*." Turn on the dramatics and demonstrate what you want them to do.

Run to another grown-up and tell them about the stranger. (If there are no other grown-ups in the house, you can substitute a teddy bear or doll as a grown up for practice sessions - just be sure your child understands that with a *real* stranger they have to tell a *real* grown-up.) Then tell your child it's their turn (taking turns makes it fun!) and have your child practice saying NO and 'running away' to tell a grown up. Prompt them with what to tell the grown up if they need it. Something along the lines of, "That stranger (or man/woman/person) wants me to find his puppy," is simple and effective, but use whatever works best for you.

Finish the session by role-playing. Have your child pretend to be the Bad Stranger (kids love this part) and ask you to help find a lost puppy. Dramatically carry out all the steps above. Then reverse rolls and let your child show you what they've learned. Hugs, giggles, and high fives all around when they get it right!

If your child is ready to move on to other activities now, that's okay. But if they are enjoying the game, you may continue practicing other scenarios. Begin each one with "What if *someone you don't know* tells you ____. What do you do?" Some common scenarios are:

I have some candy/cookies/stickers for you.

I have some kittens in the car, want to see?

Do you want to play a really cool game?

Your mom/dad told me to pick you up.

I need your help carrying these things.

When your child responds appropriately, and without prompting, to each of the above scenarios over the course of a few days, it's time to move on to the physical aspect of dealing with Bad Strangers.

7
FIGHTING BACK

Kids must be taught to fight back against Bad Strangers. Every year I am approached by parents worried that if their child tries to fight back they will get hurt. And my response is always the same. Yes, they may indeed get hurt. They may end up with a broken arm, a black eye or even worse. But which does the parent prefer - a child with a broken arm or a child to bury? The statistic I mentioned earlier bears repeating:

> Kids who walk quietly away
> often don't come home.
> Kids that fight - even little kids -
> sometimes get away.

This doesn't mean you have to sign your kids up for karate or teach them to box. (Although self-defense classes for older kids are a good idea.) It simply means that you need to spend some time teaching your child that in some circumstances - like dealing with

Bad Strangers - it is okay to fight back.

This concept is very hard for some kids. After all, they've been taught not to hit, kick, pull hair, or bite. They are told to be nice, behave, don't talk back, and do what grown-ups say. Therefore, it is _extremely important_ for parents to role-play these situations at home with their child.

Start simply, by playing the _Stranger-What If_ game from the previous chapter. Choose one of the scenarios and act it out with the parent pretending to be the Bad Stranger. But this time, take hold of your child's hand. When it comes to the part where your child should run away - do they pull their hand away and run? If so, great! If not, explain that you want them to pull their hand away and run. Then practice, but keep it light-hearted and fun.

Repeat the same scenario again, but this time hold onto your child's wrist, firmly. Don't let go easily. Make them really yank to get away. Explain that Bad Strangers might hold on really tight! Then reverse roles (remember, taking turns makes it fun for your child) and practice a few more times.

Now it's time to talk about fighting back. Again, keep it light-hearted and fun. Be dramatic! Young children learn best through play, so skip the 'parent voice' for now. (I'll let you know when to use it.) Remember, if it feels like a "lesson" kids stop paying attention.

Repeat the same scenario as earlier, but do *not* let your child pull away. Explain that sometimes, even if they pull really, really hard, they might not be able to pull their hand or arm away from a Bad Stranger. But that's okay, because there are other things they CAN do! (Leaning in close and whispering this last line really draws kids in.) Then go on and explain that they should start by screaming as loud as they can - "Help! Let go of me!" - and to keep screaming it while trying to pull away. (Again, screaming loudly is very important - it may draw the attention of others nearby.) Practice this once or twice with your child, and then ask them what else they could do if the Bad Stranger *still* doesn't let them go. Give them time to think, and listen to their answers. Some will say I don't know, but many have the right idea. If your child claims they will kick or hit the Bad Stranger, bring on the dramatics! Happy dance and high fives all around!

Don't be surprised if your child looks at you like you've lost your mind. After all they've spent their entire lives being told (by you!) not to hit or kick people. So… now is the time to pull out your 'parent voice' and emphasize that this behavior is ONLY for when a Bad Stranger is trying to take them away – not for fighting with siblings, parents, or classmates. Explain that when it comes to Bad Strangers, it's even okay to bite, pull hair, knock things over, (store displays, etc.) and even break things! And… they should keep doing those things until the Bad Stranger lets them go, or another grownup comes to help them.

Now that your child is staring at you wide-eyed and incredulous, it's time to completely blow their minds….tell them you actually *want* them to do all those things, but *only* to Bad Strangers that won't let go!

Then get right back to the fun and practice a few more scenarios where the Bad Stranger doesn't let go. Remind your child this is a *pretend* game, so they should just *pretend* to hit, kick, etc. This is hard for some kids, and you may need to give a few reminders that *real* hitting and kicking are for *real* Bad Strangers.

Whatever you do, don't skip this part of the learning process. Kids need to practice. Over and over again. Practice helps them to not panic or freeze up if they should ever encounter a similar situation. But keep in mind that practicing too long or too often is not good either. It becomes a chore. So follow your child's cues... stop when they've had enough for the day.

One special note: We've all seen kids have temper tantrums in public places. Most of us simply shake our head and walk away, glad that it's not our child having the meltdown. Those that prey on young children know this, and use it to their advantage. If approached, the predator simply explains that little Billy or little Suzy is having a temper tantrum, and then picks up the crying child and leaves. No one stops them, or even questions them. That's why it's an absolute must for you and your child to practice the following scenario occasionally. Add your own dramatics to keep it from being a 'lesson'. Your child will pay more attention, and remember it better if it's a fun conversation and activity instead of a 'talk'.

Start by explaining to your child that sometimes when another grown-up comes to help, the Bad Stranger might try to be *extra tricky*. They might lie, and tell the other grown-up that they are your mommy or daddy, and that you are just being naughty. Tell them if that ever happens, you want them to scream "Help! He's not my daddy!" (or mommy/grandpa/etc.) over and over again. Older kids can add "He's hurting me!" or "He's stealing me!"

Think about it, as a parent you've probably witnessed more than a few temper tantrums, right? Have you ever heard a child use those words during a tantrum? What if you're the bystander, witnessing what at first glance appears to be a temper tantrum, and then the child starts screaming over and over again - "Help! He's not my daddy! He's hurting me!" Aren't you going to pay more attention? Maybe even notify authorities, or jot down a license plate number? I certainly hope so.

Remember, practice helps your child learn to respond in a way that may someday save their life, but you must keep it fun for them, not frightening. Always follow your child's cues… stop when they've had enough for the day.

When you do come back to it, whether it's tomorrow, next week, or even next month, always review what they've already learned first. Then try changing up the scenarios; pick your child up instead of just grabbing their hand. What do they do? With an older child, you can even cover their mouth when they scream. (Younger kids may instinctively bite - wait until they are a bit older.) Create new scenarios, relevant to your child or location. Try scenarios with two kids. (The one being held should fight; the other should always run away, and tell a grown up right away.) As long as you keep these practice sessions light-hearted and fun, the possibilities are endless. Just be sure to emphasize (using your 'parent voice') at the end of each session that this behavior is ONLY for when a bad stranger is trying to take them away – not for fighting with siblings, parents, or classmates.

Finally, when your child has a good grasp on who a stranger is, the difference between Good Strangers and Bad Strangers, and how to fight back, it's time to celebrate! Have them call grandma or grandpa, or a favorite aunt and uncle to tell them what they've learned about strangers. Make it a big deal! Reward your child with a trip to the Dollar Store, or a favorite restaurant. Or maybe even create a sparkly glittery award for them to hang on the wall. Whatever you choose, make it special! The more excited and enthusiastic you are about their accomplishment, the better it will stick with them.

~~~~~~~~~~~~~~

As a follow up to the Stranger Danger segment of the Personal Safety unit I teach each year, I spend some time discussing the topics of Getting Lost and Good Touch/Bad Touch with the children. I've included a brief overview of both subjects in the next two chapters so that you may expand on what your child has already learned. As always, keep it light-hearted and fun, practice regularly, and make it a Big Deal when they get it right.

8
GETTING LOST

Kids never get lost; just ask them. When they are at Wal-Mart, and they turn around and mom is gone, they aren't lost – they know where they are – they're at Wal-Mart. It's their mom that's lost!

Young children have their own unique way of seeing the world, don't they? With this in mind, spend a little time now discussing with your child what to do if their grown-up gets lost.

If they are in a store, they should go straight to the check-out lady. (Check-out ladies are Good Strangers, remember?) and go right to the front of the line. Explain that when a grown-up is lost, kids get special privileges and can go straight to the front - they don't have to wait in line! They should tell the check-out lady that their mom/dad is lost. (Have them practice in a loud voice "Excuse me, my mom is lost.") The check-out lady will help them find their grown-up because that's part of their job. (Note: I use the term check-out *lady* here because that's what most young kids call a cashier. Going to a male cashier, or check-out *guy* is also acceptable.)

Also, while most kids over the age of three can easily find the check-outs, (ask your child to lead you to the check-out the next time you shop) if they can't yet do it - practice with them. Make it their job to lead the way to the check-out on every shopping trip.

Next, explain to your child that kids whose grown-ups are lost should *never* go with anyone, or talk to anyone except a check-out lady or a policeman, even if that person says they can help find their lost grown-up. This is important. Those who prey on young children look for kids who are alone or appear to be lost. They may approach the child, offer to take them to their parent, and get the child to walk calmly away with them. (Bad Strangers are tricky, remember?) For older children, you can also point out other store employees (those wearing easily identifiable uniforms and nametags) that the child can talk to if they get lost.

Then, (using your parent voice here) explain that kids should *never ever* go out into the parking lot when their grown up is lost. Lost grown-ups never go out to the car without their kids - they have to stay in the store until they are found.

Finally, talk to your child about what to do if their grown-up gets lost someplace where there are no checkouts, such as the beach or a park. Tell them they should stand still and slowly turn all the way around - looking carefully for their grown-up. If they don't spot their lost grown-up, they should then go to another _mom with kids_, and tell her their grown-up is lost. If they don't see another mom with kids, a dad with kids is okay too.

9
GOOD TOUCH/BAD TOUCH

Little kids trust adults, and love secrets. Unfortunately, that can sometimes be a dangerous combination. It's important for children to learn that sometimes it's okay to share your body – like hugging mom and dad, or kissing grandma – but that they don't have to share their body if it makes them feel uncomfortable – like someone squeezing them too tight, or touching them in places their swim suit covers.

When talking with kids about Good Touches and Bad Touches, I find it helpful to use a puppet friend to convey the message. Parents may wish to do the same. Start by introducing your puppet friend by name (mine is named Steven, but any name will do). Have the puppet explain that they want to talk to your child about something *very important* - Good Touches and Bad Touches.

The puppet (from here forward simply referred to as Steven) always starts with Good Touches. With a light-hearted and silly

attitude, he talks about hugs and backrubs,
grandma kisses and ruffling hair - having a
child demonstrate each on him. He then asks if
they can think of any other Good Touches, and
discusses each Good Touch they come up
with.

Steven then becomes more serious, and
talks about Bad Touches. He explains that bad
touches sometimes leave owies, like cuts or
bruises, and that even though sometimes
mommies and daddies might spank their child,
it's never okay for a grown-up, even a mommy
or daddy, to leave owies like he has (simulated
stitches & bruises - drawn on with a marker).
Steven says to tell a teacher, or other grown-up
they know if anyone ever gives them owies.

Then he goes on to explain another kind of
Bad Touch. He talks about everyone having
private parts, and that those parts are where a
person's swimsuit covers them. He explains
that sometimes mom or dad might help them
wipe, or wash their private parts in the bathtub,
and that sometimes doctors need to touch
private parts when kids get a checkup, but that
no one else should ever touch their private
parts. And kids should never touch anyone
else's private parts – *even if the other person*

says it's okay. Steven finishes by teaching an action chant about what to do if anyone ever tries to touch their private parts, or asks them to touch theirs.

The chant that is taught is widely used throughout stranger danger and child abuse prevention programs. It is "Say NO! Run Away! Tell a Grown-up Right Away!" Some programs present it as a song, and teach it in a quiet sing-song type of rhythm. While this may be great for very young children, I've found that most kids prefer the action chant.

To teach your child the action chant, start by standing up and having your child do the same. Then demonstrate the actions and chant in a loud voice.

"Say NO!"
(Cup hands around mouth as if cheering on a sports team)
"Run Away!"
(Run in place - fast!)
"Tell a Grown-up Right Away!"
(Cup hands around mouth on word 'Tell', point to a grown-up on the words 'grown-up', and clap hands with each syllable of 'right away'.)

Have your child join in as you repeat it several times. Then ask them to try it on their own. High fives and hugs for getting it right! Tell them to remember it, because you will be asking them again later. (Ask "What do you do if someone wants to touch your private parts?" Or "What do you do if someone wants you to touch *their* private parts?")

As in the earlier Stranger Danger sessions, ask your child one of the above questions a few times throughout the day, rewarding correct answers with excitement and high fives. Don't forget to ask them again the following morning.

When they've got it down, have them call grandma and tell her what they've learned, or demonstrate the chant to grandpa when he stops by to visit. Asking your child to teach the chant to younger siblings or friends is also a great way to reinforce what they've learned!

The Child Abuse Council also offers Good Touch/Bad Touch sessions for young children. These sessions are usually free for groups of ten or more children, and are offered in local classrooms, daycares, libraries, churches, or other places where children gather. Contact your local Child Abuse Council to learn more.

In addition to talking with your child about good touch/bad touch issues, parents may wish to visit the website

http://familywatchdog.us/.

This will link you to the sex offender list. Type in your address/zip, and a map will appear showing the homes and workplaces of sex offenders near you. Additional links will give you their crime/convictions and photos.

10
A FINAL REMINDER

Personal safety is an important topic for parents to discuss with their kids on a regular basis. Please, speak openly with your kids about strangers and personal safety often. Use and expand on the information I've given here, practice the what-if scenarios, and use teachable moments to reinforce those lessons. Above all else, remember that young children learn best through play. So even though you may feel silly, occasionally spend some time playing 'stranger' with your child. Make it engaging, keep it positive, and the lessons will be remembered for years to come.

###

A NOTE FROM THE AUTHOR

Word -of-mouth is crucial for any author to succeed, and Independent Authors need readers like you to get the word out about their books. If you enjoyed this book, please consider leaving a review at Amazon.com, even if it's only a line or two; it really does make a difference, and would be very much appreciated. Simply go to www.amazon.com, and type Kristi Porter into the search bar. Then choose the appropriate story, click reviews, and create your own review.

~ ~ ~

If you would like to receive an automatic email when my next book is released, go to http://eepurl.com/ES3kD to sign up. Your email address will never be shared and you can unsubscribe at any time.

~ ~ ~

Thanks so much for taking the time to read and review my work. It's readers like you that help make my next book even better!

Kristi Porter

ABOUT THE AUTHOR

Kristi Porter has over twenty-five years of experience working with young children, both as a preschool teacher, and as an award winning child care provider. She holds a degree in Early Childhood Education and Development, as well as a national Child Development Associate Credential. In 1999, she was awarded the Governor's Quality Care Award for her outstanding commitment to the care and education of young children.

Always a reader, Kristi never thought much about writing until she entered a writing contest sponsored by the Detroit Free Press. Her story - *The Worst Vacation Ever* - went on to be published in a travel anthology that was distributed worldwide. This was followed by numerous articles published in local magazines and newspapers. As her love of writing grew, she added adult fiction, how-to books for parents, and short humor pieces to her repertoire.

But kids and writing aren't all Kristi relishes. She also enjoys bicycling, video games, photography, Facebook, and spending time with family. She lives in Michigan.

~~~~~~~~~~~

CONNECT WITH KRISTI ONLINE

Twitter: @KristiPorter3
Facebook: Facebook/Kristi Porter -Author
Website: http://happikamper.weebly.com
Email: Kristiporter03@gmail.com

OTHER TITLES BY KRISTI PORTER

Sweet Revenge

Is Somebody Bleeding?

Martini's and Weed Whackers

Sooner or Later…You Will Get Caught

Pedaling My Ass Off - A Weight Loss Story, Well, Kinda…

Priceless Proverbs. Funny Happens When Kids Finish Famous Sayings

Priceless Proverbs 2. Funny Happens When Kids Finish Famous Sayings

Babies Come From… Where?!? Funny Happens When Kids Explain Pregnancy & Birth

How to Tell When You're Really Old! Funny Happens When Kids Define Old Age

Coming in 2015
Overheard in the Classroom

PARENT RESOURCES

Local Resources

The Child Abuse Council offers Good Touch/Bad Touch sessions for young children. These sessions are usually free for groups of ten or more children, and are offered in local classrooms, daycares, libraries, churches, or other places where children gather. Contact your local Child Abuse Council to learn more.

Many local police departments offer Stranger Danger programs for kids. While many of these programs are aimed at older children, some also offer programs for preschoolers. Contact your local police department to find out.

Books for Young Children

Not Everyone Is Nice: Helping Children Learn Caution with Strangers - by Frederick Alimonti, Ann Tedesco Ph.D., & Erik DePrince

The Berenstain Bears Learn About Strangers -

by Stan & Jan Berenstain

The Reluctantly Written but Absolutely
Necessary Book for Todays Boys and Girls -
by Patricia Stirnkorb & Claudia Wolf

It's My Body (Children's Safety & Abuse
Prevention) - by Lory Britain

Those are MY Private Parts - by Diane Hansen

I Said No! A kid-to-kid guide to keeping your
private parts private - by Kimberly King &
Sue Rama

Video: The Safe Side - Stranger Safety: Hot
Tips to Keep Cool Kids Safe with People They
Don't Know and Kinda Know (2005)

~~~~~

**Parents are also encouraged to go to
http://www.kidpower.org/ for additional
resources on the following topics:**

- •Protecting Children from
  Abduction/Kidnapping

- •Safety with Strangers and People Children Know

- •Resisting the "Illusion of Safety"

- •What Adults Need to Know About Personal Safety for Children

- •Is YOUR Child Prepared to Avoid and Escape From Danger? Free Safety Checklist for Kids On Their Way to School

- •What Children Need to Know if They Cannot Get Away at First

- •How to Pick a Good Self-Defense Program

- •Tools for Empowering Children to Explore Their   World with Safety and Confidence

- • Child Abuse Prevention in Youth Sports

- • Worthy of Trust: What Organizations Must Do to Protect Children From Harm

- • Why Affection and Teasing Should be a Child's Choice

- • Safety Tips: Protecting Children from Sexual Abuse

- • Sometimes the People Kids Love Have Problems – What Children Do and Do

NOT Need to Know

- What if a Sex Offender is Living in Our Neighborhood?

- Four Strategies for Protecting Kids From Sexual Predators

- Teaching Children About Safe and Unsafe Secrets

- Touch in Healthy Relationships

CPSIA information can be obtained at www.ICGtesting.com
Printed in the USA
LVOW04s0034240615

443540LV00030BA/1619/P

9 780615 890432